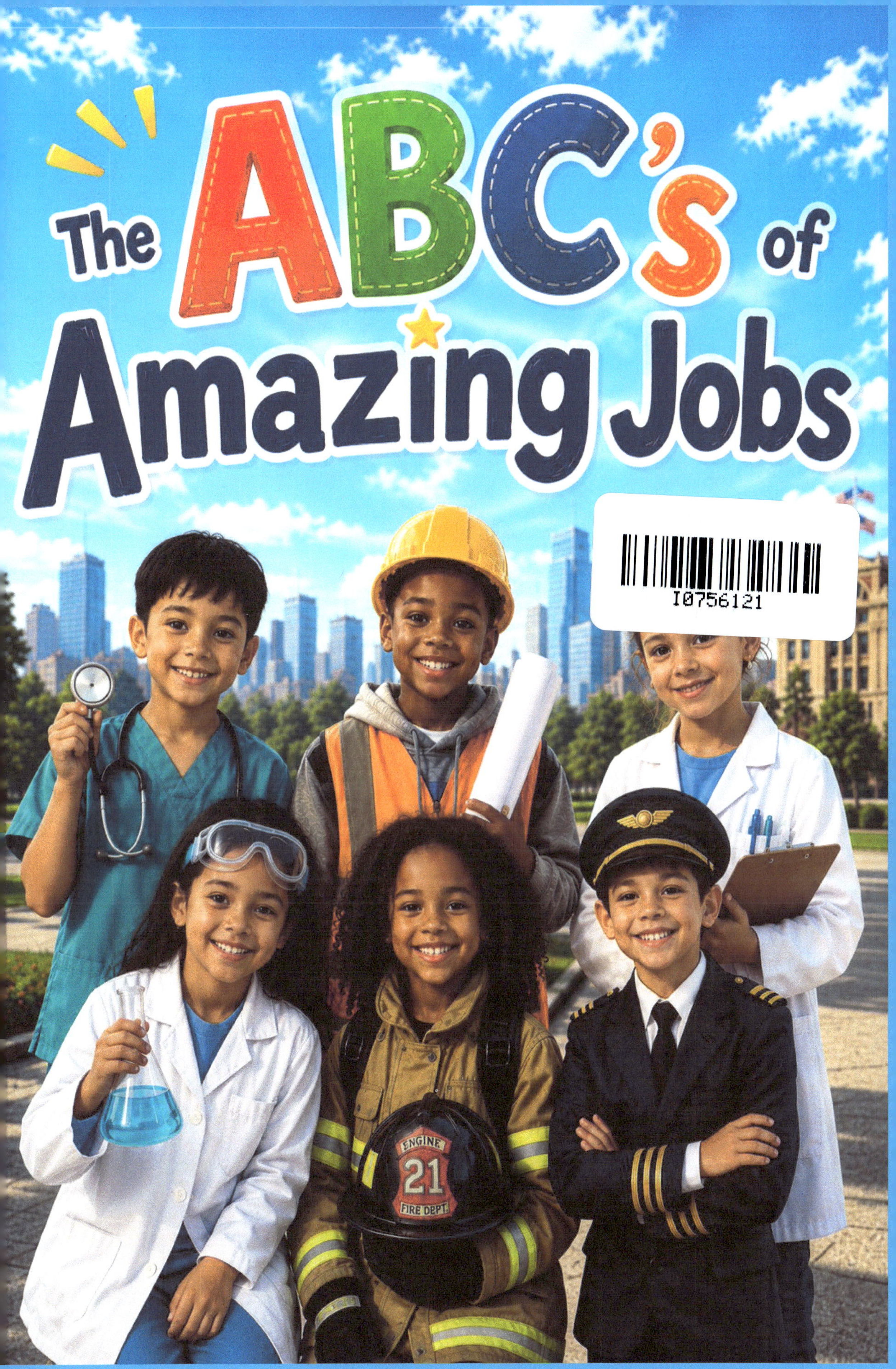
The ABC's of
Amazing Jobs
I0756121
ENGINE
21
FIRE DEPT.

BK Royston Publishing LLC

Jeffersonville, IN

http://www.bkroystonpublishing.com

bkroystonpublishing@gmail.com

ISBN: 978-1-971868-38-7

Hardback ISBN: 978-1-971868-39-4

Printed in the USA

Aa—Astronaut

Bb—Baker

Cc—Carpenter

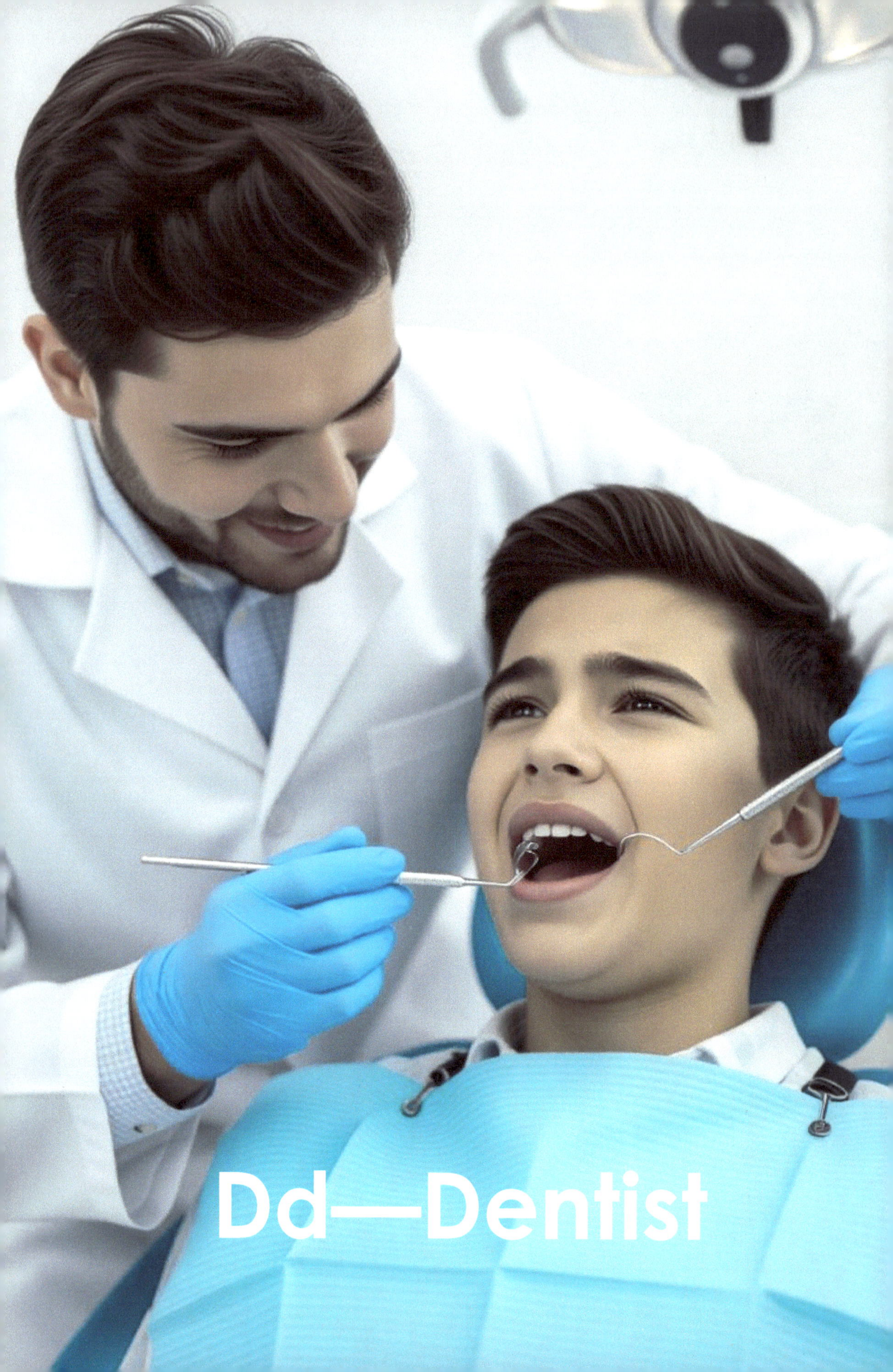
Dd—Dentist

Ee lectrician

Ff—Firefighter

Gg—Gardener

Hh—Hair Stylist

Ii—Interior Designer

Jj—Judge

Kk-Karate Instructor

Ll-Locomotive Engineer

Mm-Mechanic

Nn—Nutritionist

Oo-Optician

Pp-Pharmacist

Qq-Quality Analyst

Rr—Radiologist

Ss—Soldier

Tt-Teacher

Uu—Umpire

Vv—Veterinarian

Ww-Warehouse Technician

Xx-X-Ray Technician

Yy-Yoga Instructor

Zz—Zoologist

WHAT DO YOU WANT TO DO ONE DAY?

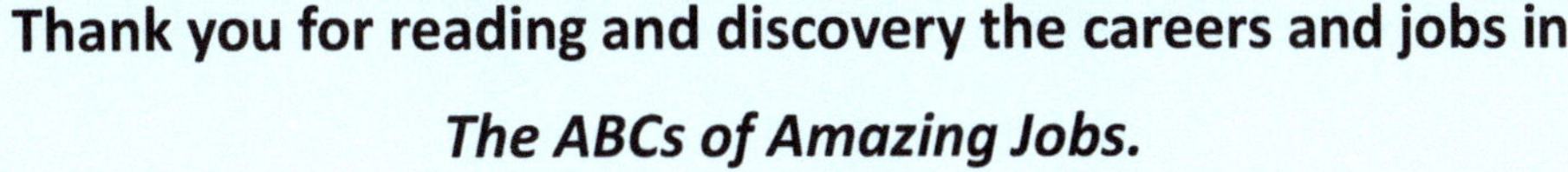

Thank you for reading and discovery the careers and jobs in

The ABCs of Amazing Jobs.

I challenge you to visit the following website and find out more information about the jobs listed.

More information visit: https://www.bls.gov/ooh/

What Amount of Education is Needed?

____

____

What Do They Do Each Day?

____

____

Where Do They Work?

____

____

How Much Money Do They Make?

____

What are other things does this job require?

____

____

____

____

WHAT DO YOU WANT TO DO ONE DAY?

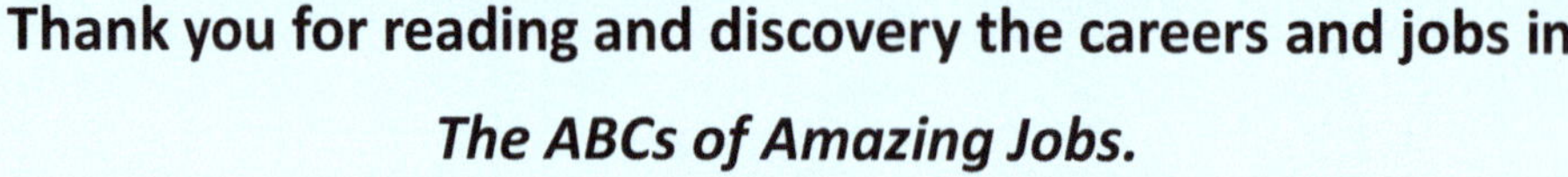

Thank you for reading and discovery the careers and jobs in

The ABCs of Amazing Jobs.

I challenge you to visit the following website and find out more information about the jobs listed.

More information visit: https://www.bls.gov/ooh/

What Amount of Education is Needed?

____

____

What Do They Do Each Day?

____

____

Where Do They Work?

____

____

How Much Money Do They Make?

____

What are other things does this job require?

____

____

____

____

About the Author

Julia Royston spends her days doing what she loves, writing, publishing, speaking about her why and motto, "Helping You Get Your Message to the Masses, Turn Your Words into Wealth and Be a Book Business Boss." Julia is the author of 150+ books, published 500+, recorded 3 music CDs and coached others to be published authors and business owners. She is the owner of five companies, a non-profit organization and the editor of the Book Business Boss Magazine.

To stay connected with Julia, visit www.juliaakroyston.com.

More Books by Julia A Royston

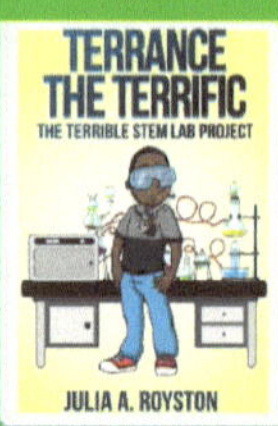

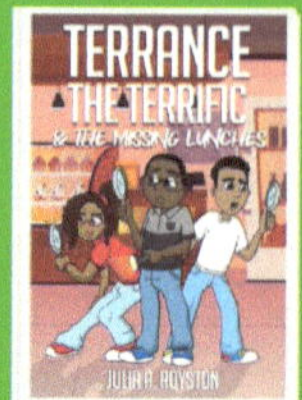

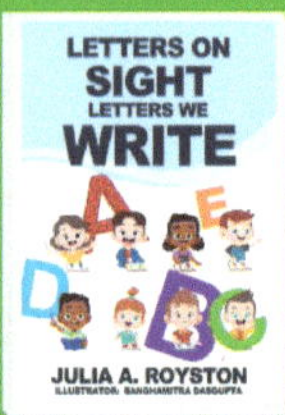

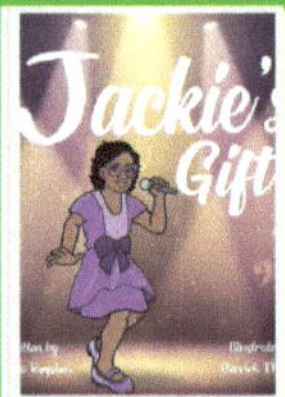

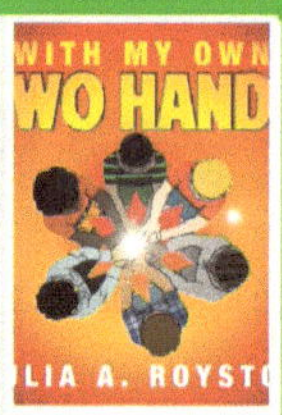

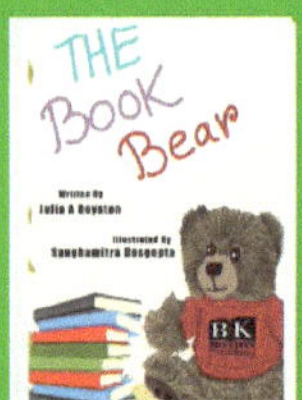

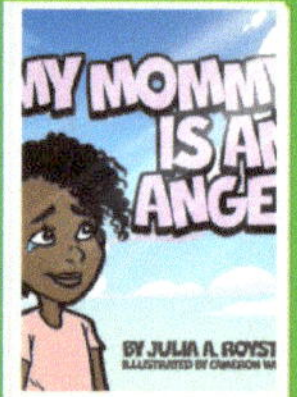

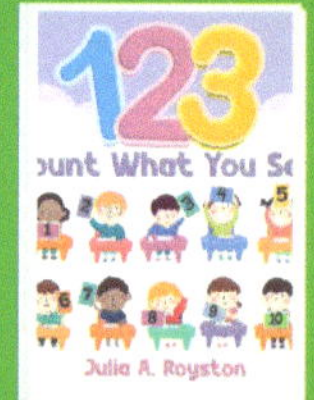

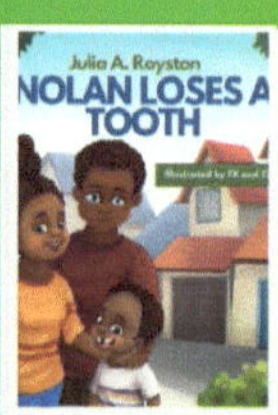

Julia Royston Books

www.roystonchildrenbookstore.com

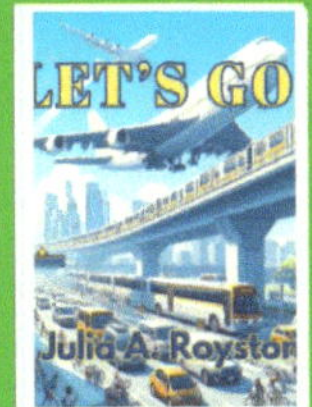
LET'S GO
Julia A. Royston

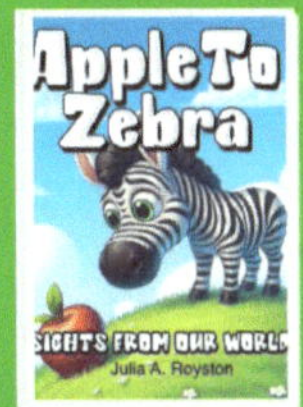
Apple To
Zebra
Julia A. Royston

LONDON

POWER IN
MY WORDS

POWER IN
MY WORDS

PODER EN MIS
PALABRAS

Sights
From Our
World
Julia A. Royston

IDEA
THINK
CREATE

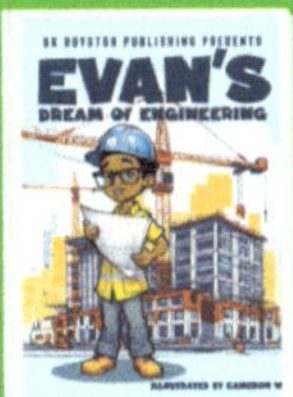
EVAN'S
DREAM OF ENGINEERING

LEAH
THE FUTURE LAWYER
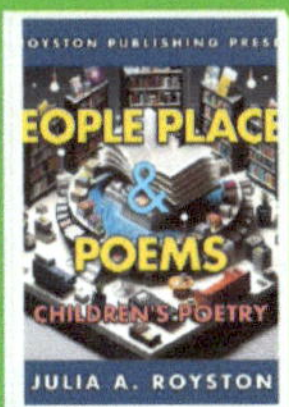
POEMS
CHILDREN'S POETRY
JULIA A. ROYSTON

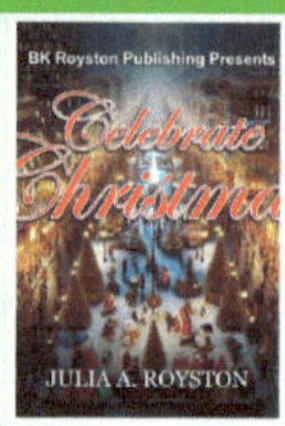

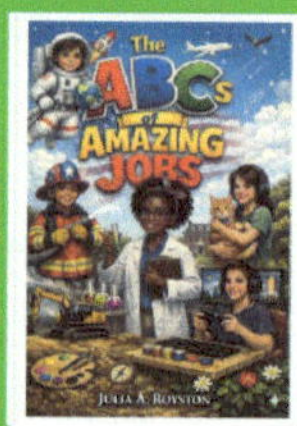

Coming Soon!

Coming Soon!

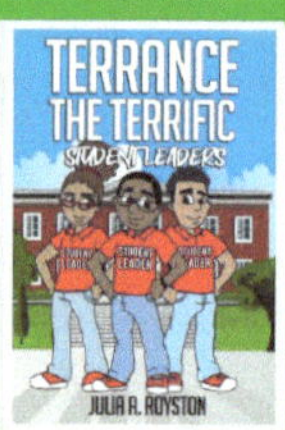

Julia Royston Books

www.roystonchildrenbookstore.com

www.ingramcontent.com/pod-product-compliance
Lightning Source LLC
LaVergne TN
LVHW070202110826
845147LV00002B/476